A
Prayer Book
with Communion Rite

ST PAULS

Prayer is our constant, indestructible link with God— our insight that can take us to Him wherever we are so that we may adore, petition, give thanks and express sorrow.

This little book of prayers was prepared to help you turn your thoughts to God and to let you know that you are in the thoughts and prayers of many.

Rev. Jerome Duesman
Sarah Watson Pendergast

With Ecclesiastical Approval

Visit our web site at
www.albahouse.org
(for orders www.alba-house.com)
or call 1-800-343-2522 (ALBA)
and request current catalog

CONTENTS

SIGN OF THE CROSS

In the name of the Father, and of the Son, and of the Holy Spirit. Amen.

THE CREED

I believe in God, the Father Almighty, Creator of heaven and earth; and in Jesus Christ, His only Son, our Lord: Who was conceived by the Holy Spirit, born of the Virgin Mary; suffered under Pontius Pilate, was crucified, died and was buried. He descended into hell; the third day He rose again from the dead; He ascended into heaven, is seated at the right hand of God the Father Almighty; from thence

He shall come to judge the living and the dead. I believe in the Holy Spirit, the Holy Catholic Church, the communion of Saints, the forgiveness of sins, the resurrection of the body, and life everlasting. Amen.

THE LORD'S PRAYER

Our Father, who art in heaven, hallowed be thy name; thy kingdom come; thy will be done on earth as it is in heaven. Give us this day our daily bread; and forgive us our trespasses as we forgive those who trespass against us; and lead us not into temptation, but deliver us from evil. Amen.

THE HAIL MARY

Hail, Mary, full of grace; the Lord is with thee: blessed art thou amongst women, and blessed is the Fruit of thy womb, Jesus.
Holy Mary, Mother of God, pray for us sinners, now and at the hour of our death. Amen.

THE GLORY BE

Glory be to the Father, and to the Son and to the Holy Spirit. As it was in the beginning, is now, and ever shall be, world without end. Amen.

MORNING OFFERING

O Jesus, through the Immaculate

Heart of Mary, I offer You my prayers, works, joys and sufferings of this day, in union with the Holy Sacrifice of the Mass throughout the world. I offer them for all the intentions of Your Sacred Heart; the salvation of souls, reparation for sin, the reunion of all Christians. I offer them for the intentions of our Bishops and of all Apostolates of Prayer, and in particular for those recommended by our Holy Father this month.

ACT OF FAITH

O my God, I firmly believe that You are one God in three divine persons, Father, Son and Holy

Spirit. I believe that Your divine Son became man and died for our sins and that He will come to judge the living and the dead. I believe these and all the truths which the Holy Catholic Church teaches and believes because You have revealed them, Who can neither deceive nor be deceived.

ACT OF HOPE

O my God, relying on Your infinite goodness and promises I hope to obtain the pardon of my sins, the help of Your grace, and life everlasting through the merits of Jesus Christ, my Lord and Redeemer.

ACT OF LOVE

O my God, I love You above
all things with my whole heart
and soul because You are all
good and worthy of all my love.
I love my neighbor as myself
for the love of You. I forgive all
who have offended me and I ask
pardon of all whom I have offended.

ACT OF CONTRITION

O my God, I am heartily sorry
for having offended You, and
I detest all my sins, because I
dread the loss of heaven and the
pains of hell; but most of all, because they offend You, my God,
Who are all good and deserving

10

of all my love. I firmly resolve, with the help of Your grace, to confess my sins, to do penance, and to amend my life. Amen.

TO THE GUARDIAN ANGEL

Angel of God, my guardian dear, to whom His love entrusts me here, ever this day be at my side, to light and guard, to rule and guide. Amen.

THE ANGELUS

(Recited after morning prayers, after Mass and before the mid-day meal)

The angel of the Lord declared unto Mary: And she conceived of the Holy Spirit.
Hail Mary …

Behold the handmaid of the Lord:
Be it done unto me according to Your word.
Hail Mary …
And the Word was made flesh;
And dwelt among us.
Hail Mary …
Pray for us, O Holy Mother of God: That we may be made worthy of the promises of Christ.

Let us pray:
Pour forth, we beg You, O Lord, Your grace into our hearts, that we to whom the Incarnation of Your Son was made known by the message of an angel, may by His passion and death be brought to the glory of His Resurrection, through the same Christ our

12

Lord. Amen.

THE QUEEN OF HEAVEN
(Replaces the Angelus during Easter time)

Queen of heaven, rejoice,
Alleluia! For He, Whom you
merited to bear, Alleluia!
Has risen as He said, Alleluia!
Pray for us to God, Alleluia!
Rejoice and be glad, O Virgin
Mary, Alleluia! For our Lord is
truly risen, Alleluia!

Let us pray:
O God, Who by the Resurrection of Your Son, our Lord, Jesus Christ, was pleased to make glad the whole world, grant, we beseech You, that through the intercession of the Virgin

Mary, we may attain to the joys of eternal life, through the same Christ our Lord. Amen.

GRACE BEFORE MEALS

Bless us, O Lord, and these Your gifts which we are about to receive from Your goodness, through Christ our Lord. Amen.

GRACE AFTER MEALS

We give You thanks, Almighty God, for these and all Your benefits Who live and reign world without end. Amen. May the Divine Assistance remain always with us, and may the souls of the faithful departed through

the mercy of God, rest in peace.
Amen.

PRAYER FOR
OUR HOLY FATHER

O God, the Shepherd and Ruler
of all Your faithful people, mer-
cifully look upon Your servant,
N..., our Pope, whom You have
chosen as the chief shepherd
to preside over Your Church;
grant him, we beg You, so to
edify those under his care, that
he may attain life everlasting
together with his flock, through
Christ our Lord. Amen.

PRAYER
TO THE HOLY SPIRIT

Come Holy Spirit, fill the hearts of Your faithful, and enkindle in them the fire of Your love. Send forth Your Spirit and they shall be created and You shall renew the face of the earth.

O God, Who has taught the hearts of the faithful by the light of the Holy Spirit, grant that by the gift of the same Spirit we may be always truly wise, and ever rejoice in His consolations, through Christ our Lord. Amen.

PRAYERS
BEFORE COMMUNION

ACT OF FAITH

O Jesus, I believe that You are the Christ, the Son of the Living God, Who came on earth to save man from sin. I believe, also, that in receiving the Holy Eucharist I shall receive Your Body and Blood. I believe this firmly because You are almighty and You have said it.

ACT OF DESIRE

O Jesus, my God, I wish with all my heart to receive You. Come into my poor soul, O Jesus, come with Your Body and Blood, Your

Soul and Divinity, so that I may have You living in me, and may live for You and with You forever. Amen.

AN ACT
OF CONSECRATION

O Sacred Heart of Jesus, filled with infinite love, broken by my ingratitude, pierced by my sins, yet loving me still: accept the consecration that I make to You of all that I am and all that I have. Take every faculty of my soul and body. Draw me, day by day, nearer and nearer to Your Sacred Heart, and there, as I can bear the lesson, teach me Your blessed ways. Amen.

ADMINISTRATION OF COMMUNION TO THE SICK BY AN EXTRAORDINARY MINISTER

GREETING

Minister says:
Peace to this house and to all who live in it.

PENITENTIAL RITE:

Minister says:
My brothers and sisters, to prepare ourselves for this celebration, let us call to mind our sins. (Pause)

All say:

I confess to almighty God, and to you, my brothers and sisters, that I have sinned through my own fault in my thoughts and in

19

my words, in what I have done, and in what I have failed to do; and I ask blessed Mary, ever virgin, all the angels and saints, and you, my brothers and sisters, to pray for me to the Lord our God.

Minister says:
May almighty God have mercy on us, forgive us our sins, and bring us to everlasting life.

All respond:
Amen.

THE READING OF THE WORD
JOHN 6:54-58

He who feeds on my flesh and drinks my blood has life eternal, and I will raise him up on the last day. For my flesh is real food and my blood real drink. The man who feeds on my flesh and drinks my blood remains in me, and I in him.

20

Just as the Father who has life sent me and I have life because of the Father, so the man who feeds on me will have life because of me. This is the bread that came down from heaven. Unlike your ancestors who ate and died nonetheless, the man who feeds on this bread shall live forever.

Or JOHN 14:6

Jesus told him: "I am the way, and the truth, and the life; no one comes to the Father but through me."

Or JOHN 14:23

Jesus answered: "Anyone who loves me will be true to my word, and my Father will love him; we will come to him and make our dwelling place with him."

HOLY COMMUNION

Minister says:
Now let us pray together to the Father

in the words given us by our Lord Jesus Christ.

All say:

Our Father, who art in heaven, hallowed be thy name; thy kingdom come; thy will be done on earth as it is in heaven. Give us this day our daily bread; and forgive us our trespasses as we forgive those who trespass against us; and lead us not into temptation, but deliver us from evil. Amen.

Minister says:
This is the Lamb of God who takes away the sins of the world. Happy are those who are called to his supper.

All respond:

Lord, I am not worthy to receive

you, but only say the word and I shall be healed.

Minister says:
The body of Christ.

You respond:

Amen.

Minister says:
God our Father, almighty and eternal, we confidently call upon you, that the body (and blood) of Christ which our brother (sister) has received may bring him (her) lasting health in mind and body. We ask this through Christ our Lord.

All respond:

Amen.

OR:
Lord, you have nourished us with one

bread from heaven. Fill us with your Spirit, and make us one in peace and love. We ask this through Christ our Lord.

All respond:

Amen.

CONCLUDING RITE

Minister says:
May the Lord bless us, protect us from all evil and bring us to everlasting life.

OR:

May the almighty and merciful God bless and protect us, the Father, and the Son, and the Holy Spirit.

All respond:

Amen.

THANKSGIVING PRAYER AFTER COMMUNION

THE "ANIMA CHRISTI"

Soul of Christ, sanctify me.
Body of Christ, save me.
Blood of Christ, inebriate me.
Water from the side of Christ,
wash me.
Passion of Christ, strengthen me.
Good Jesus, listen to me.
Within Your wounds hide me.
Never permit me to be separated
from You.
From the evil one protect me.
At the hour of my death call me,
And bid me come to You,
That with Your saints I may praise
You for ever and ever. Amen.

PRAYERS
AFTER COMMUNION

O my Jesus, Whom I have received this day into my soul, fill me with Your love and Your grace as You have filled me with Your presence, and grant me the assistance to remain always united to You in mind and in body.

O my Jesus, Who in this sacrament have given me Yourself and have commemorated Your Holy Passion, fill my soul with grace and grant unto me, in this sacrament, Your pledge of future glory.

PRAYER
BEFORE A CRUCIFIX

Good and gentle Jesus, I humbly
kneel in Your sight, and with the
most fervent desire of my soul
I pray and beg You to impress
upon my heart lively sentiments
of faith, hope and charity; true
repentance for my sins and a
most firm purpose of amendment.

27

With great love and tender pity I consider within myself and contemplate Your five most precious wounds, having before my eyes that which David, the prophet, long ago spoke in Your own Person concerning You, my Jesus: "They have pierced My hands and My feet; They have numbered all My bones." Amen.

DEVOTIONS TO THE SACRED HEART OF JESUS

O Heart of love, I put all my trust in You; for I fear all things from my own weakness, but I hope for all things from Your goodness. Most sweet Heart of

Jesus, grant that peace, the fruit of justice and charity, may reign throughout the world.

O most holy Heart of Jesus, fountain of every blessing, I adore You, I love You, and with a lively sorrow for my sins, I offer You this poor heart of mine. Make me humble, patient, pure and wholly obedient to Your will. Grant, good Jesus, that I may live in You and for You. Protect me in the midst of danger; comfort me in my afflictions; give me health of body, assistance in my temporal needs, Your blessing on all that I do, and the grace of a holy death. Amen.

MEMORARE

Remember, most gracious Virgin Mary, that never was it known, that anyone who prayed for your protection, implored your help, and sought your intercession, was left unaided. Inspired with this confidence, I hasten to you, O virgin of virgins, my mother. To you I come; before you I stand, sinful and sorrowful. O mother of the Word Incarnate, do not ignore my petitions, but in your mercy hear and answer me. Amen.

DEVOTIONS TO THE BLESSED VIRGIN MARY

HAIL HOLY QUEEN

Hail, Holy Queen, Mother of mercy, hail, our life, our sweetness, and our hope! To you do we cry, poor banished children of Eve! To you do we send up our sighs, mourning and weeping in this vale of tears! Turn, then, most gracious advocate, your eyes of mercy towards us; and after this our exile, show us the blessed fruit of your womb, Jesus! O clement, O loving, O sweet Virgin Mary!

V. Pray for us, O holy Mother of God.
R. That we may become worthy of the promises of Christ.

PRAYER
AFTER THE ROSARY

Let us pray.

O God, by the life, death and resurrection of Your only-begotten Son, You purchased for us the rewards of eternal life; grant, we beseech You, that while meditating on these mysteries of the Holy Rosary, we may imitate what they contain and obtain what they promise. Through the same Christ our Lord. Amen.

NOVENA OF OUR MOTHER OF PERPETUAL HELP

Virgin Mother of Christ, assist the needy who resort to you.

Give comfort to all who trust in your help.

Let us pray. O Lord Jesus Christ, we venerate the wondrous picture of Your Mother Mary. You gave her to be our mother also, always ready to help us. Grant that we who earnestly implore her motherly assistance may be worthy to enjoy the eternal fruit of Your redemption. You live and reign for ever and ever. Amen.

THE MAGNIFICAT

My soul magnifies the Lord,
   and my spirit rejoices in God
   my Savior
Because He has regarded the

lowliness of His handmaid;
for behold henceforth
all generations shall
call me blessed;
Because He Who is mighty has
done great things for me,
and holy is His name;
And His mercy is from
generation to generation
on those who fear Him.
He has shown might with His
arm; He has scattered the
proud in the conceit of
their heart.
He has put down the mighty
from their thrones, and has
exalted the lowly,
He has filled the hungry with
good things, and the rich He

has sent away empty.
He has given help to Israel, His
   servant, mindful of His mercy.
Even as He spoke to our fathers,
   to Abraham and to his
   posterity forever.

PRAYER OF SELF-OFFERING

Take, O Lord, all my liberty.
Receive my memory, my under-
standing and my will. You have
given me all that I am and all
that I possess. I return it all to
You and surrender it to the guid-
ance of Your will. Give me only
Your love and grace. With these
I am rich enough and ask for
nothing more.
   Spiritual Exercises, St. Ignatius of Loyola

PRAYER
FOR A SICK PERSON

O God, who bestowed on St. Gerard the power of healing all kinds of infirmities, glorify him, who was so merciful toward human misery, by delivering me from my present sickness. Grant also that, being strengthened in body, I may take greater care to avoid sin and overcome my evil passions, the spiritual disease that drags so many to everlasting death. I ask this through Christ our Lord. Amen.

PRAYER IN AFFLICTION

Keep me from bitterness. It is so easy to nurse sharp bitter thoughts each dull dark hour! Against self-pity, Man of Sorrows, defend me with Your deep sweetness and Your gentle power! Help me to harvest a new sympathy for suffering human-kind, a wiser pity for those who lift a heavier cross with You.

PRAYER WHEN SUFFERING

Sweet Jesus — May Your own patient, loving Heart teach me to accept suffering, and to prize highly every thorn You give me from Your crown, every splinter of Your Sacred Cross. O Most Loving Heart of Jesus, You Who are the fruitful source of all graces, imprint in my heart a most perfect love of You, and of Your dear Mother Mary — an ardent love for my neighbor, an entire resignation to Your Most Holy Will — a contempt for worldly pleasures, and a happy passage to the eternity of Paradise.

PRAYER FOR DECEASED

Our Father in Heaven, we ask You to bless us, the poor in spirit and grant us Your consolation. We ask that You look favorably upon Your son (or daughter), who has left this world and grant him (her) peace and eternal life with You in Heaven. For the Lord said, I am the resurrection and the life, he who believes in Me will not die forever.

Lord, grant us all the grace to rejoice with You and the angels that Your faithful servant has been taken up to Heaven. For death in this world is only the beginning of eternal joy and happiness made possible by the death and resurrection of Your Son Jesus Christ our Lord. Amen.

Eternal rest grant unto them, O Lord, and let perpetual light shine upon them. May they rest in peace. Amen.

PRAYER TO ST. JOSEPH
FOR THE DYING

Everlasting Father, for the sake of Your love for St. Joseph, who was Your most faithful Guardian upon earth, have mercy on us and on those who are dying.

OUR FATHER...
HAIL MARY...
GLORY BE TO THE FATHER...

PRAYER
FOR A HAPPY DEATH

Holy Father, St. Francis, who died longing for God, I invite you, with Jesus and Mary, to assist me at the hour of my death. Be then to me a father and protector, and intercede for me that

I may die in the grace of God
and deserve to dwell in Heaven,
where you now enjoy everlasting glory. Amen.

PSALM 23

The Lord is my shepherd;
   I shall not want.
In verdant pastures
   He gives me repose;
Beside restful waters
   He leads me;
   He refreshes my soul.
He guides me in right paths
   for His name's sake.
Even though I walk
   in the dark valley
I fear no evil; for
   You are at my side

With Your rod and Your staff
  that give me courage.
You spread the table before me
  in the sight of my foes;
You anoint my head with oil;
  my cup overflows.
Only goodness and kindness
  follow me all the days
  of my life;
And I shall dwell
  in the house of the Lord
  for years to come.

PRAYER FOR PEACE

O God, from Whom proceed
all holy desires, all right coun-
sels and just works, grant unto
us Your servants that peace
which the world cannot give,

that our hearts may be devoted to Your service, and that, being delivered from the fear of our enemies, we may pass our time in peace under Your protection. Through Christ our Lord. Amen.

PRAYER OF
ST. FRANCIS OF ASSISI

Lord, make me an instrument of
Your peace!
Where there is hatred,
let me sow Love;
Where there is injury, Pardon;
Where there is doubt, Faith;
Where there is despair, Hope;
Where there is sadness, Joy.
O Divine Master,

Grant that I may not so much
　　seek to be consoled
　　as to console,
　　to be understood
　　as to understand,
　　to be loved as to love;
For it is in giving that we receive;
　　it is in pardoning
　　that we are pardoned;
And it is in dying that
　　we are born to Eternal Life.

PSALM FOR MATURE YEARS

You are my hope, O Lord;
　　my trust, O God, from
　　my youth.
On You I depend from birth;
　　from my mother's womb

You are my strength;
constant has been my hope
in You.
Cast me not off in my old age;
as my strength fails,
forget me not.
O God, You have taught me
from my youth, and till
the present I proclaim
Your wondrous deeds;
And now that I am old and gray,
O God, forsake me not
Till I proclaim Your strength
to every generation that
is to come.
Though You have made me feel
many bitter afflictions,
You will again revive me;
from the depths of the earth
You will once more raise me.

(From Psalm 71)

EVENING PRAYER

May He support us all day long,
Till the shades lengthen
   and the evening comes,
And the busy world is hushed;
And the fever of life is over,
And our work is done.
Then in His mercy may He
give us a safe lodging and a
holy rest and peace at the last.
(John Henry Cardinal Newman)

The Lord bless you
   and keep you
May His face shine upon you
   and be gracious to you.
May He look upon you
   with kindness
   and give you His peace.
(Numbers 6:24-26)

SOURCES

Sign of the Cross: Key of the Kingdom, Imprimatur, Most Reverend Francis J. Mugavero, DD, Bishop of Brooklyn, New York (Printed in Belgium)

The Creed: (same as above)

The Lord's Prayer: (same as above)

The Hail Mary: (same as above)

The Glory Be: (same as above)

Morning Offering: Montserrat Women's Auxiliary, Montserrat, Lake Dallas, Texas

Act of Faith: (same as above)

Act of Hope: (same as above)

Act of Love: (same as above)

Act of Contrition: (same as above)

The Angelus: (same as above)

The Queen of Heaven: My Favorite Prayers and Reflections, Daughters of St. Paul, 50 St. Paul's Avenue, Boston, MA 02130

Grace Before Meals: Montserrat Women's Auxiliary, Montserrat, Lake Dallas, Texas (same as above)

Grace After Meals: (same as above)

Prayer For Our Holy Father: (same as above)

Prayers To The Holy Spirit: Adapted from My Prayer Book, Father Lasance, Benziger Brothers, New York, Cincinnati, Chicago

Prayers Before Communion, Act of Faith: The Greatest Prayer, The Mass, Bruce Publishing Co., Milwaukee

Act of Desire: (same as above)

Act of Consecration: Psalms, Prayers, Praise, Sacred Heart League, Walls, Mississippi 38680

Thanksgiving Prayer After Communion, Anima Christi: Montserrat Women's Auxiliary (same as above)

Prayers After Communion: The Devotion of Our Time, Sacred Heart League, Walls, Mississippi 38680

Prayer Before a Crucifix: Montserrat Women's Auxiliary (same as above)

Devotions To the Sacred Heart of Jesus: Key of the Kingdom (same as above)

Memorare: Montserrat Women's Auxiliary (same as above)

Hail Holy Queen: Key of the Kingdom (same as above)

Novena of Our Mother of Perpetual Help: (same as above)

The Magnificat: (same as above)

Prayer After the Rosary: (same as above)

Prayer for a Sick Person: (same as above)

Prayer in Affliction: (same as above)

Prayer When Suffering: (same as above)

Prayer For Deceased: (same as above)

Prayer to St. Joseph for the Dying: (same as above)

Psalm 23: Psalms, Prayers, Praise (same as above)

Prayer of St. Francis of Assisi: Psalms, Prayers, Praise (same as above)

Psalm for Mature Years: (same as above)

Evening Prayer: (same as above)

St. Francis' Blessing: Franciscan Mission Associates, Mount Vernon, NY

Administration of Communion to the Sick by an Extraordinary Minister: International Committee on English in the Liturgy